Riddles

The 100 Best "What Am I?" Riddles Ever Made

Charles Berry

SOUTHSHORE
PUBLICATIONS & DISTRIBUTION

www.southshorepublications.com

INTRODUCTION

Hello and welcome to my book on Riddles. Inside you will find 100 of the greatest riddles in the world. I have always been fascinated by riddles and brain teasers ever since reading the Riddles in the Dark chapter from The Hobbit by J. R. R. Tolkien as a child. So it's safe to say I have heard my fair share!

The riddles in this book are all of the "What am I?" variety. Meaning you will get some clues as to what exactly is describing itself, in a cryptic manner of course, then you will have to decipher what exactly it is.

These are some of my personal favorites, although I did try to pick ones that were not only very clever, but also less common than some of the general riddles that most people know. So chances are, you won't have heard too many of these before.

I have laid the book out with the riddle on one page and the answer on the other. This ensures you can't glance at the answer without first turning the page and therefore removes the temptation to spoil it for yourself!

Just so you can get a better idea of how the riddles are laid out and solved, here are a couple of examples for you to take a look at:

"My thunder comes before my lightning and cloud, my rains are dry, I stand tall and proud."

Did you get it? The answer is a volcano. The thunder is the rumbling of the volcano, the rain is the ash that falls, etc.

Let's try one more example before we get started for those of you who haven't had much practice at riddles, because some of the riddles in this book are kind of tough:

"You put me in dry and I come out wet. The longer you leave me, the stronger I get."

That's a bit of a tougher one. The answer is a teabag. That one's quite self-explanatory. If you think about it, as long as you consider things that it gets stronger the longer you leave it, combined with the fact that you know liquid is involved, it's not too hard to work out! Of course it easy to say that when you know the answer!

Anyway, enjoy the book and good luck!

I cannot be stolen, but I can be

given out. I am owned by all,

those with too little have doubt.

What am I?

Knowledge.

Sometimes I fly, sometimes I drag on. One thing I know, is that you will miss me when I am gone. What am I?

Time.

I jump when I run, I sit when I stand. A pocket of life, gives me a helping hand. What am I?

A Kangaroo.

I will not break, if thrown from a great height. But I will burst into flame if you set me alight. What am I?

A Tissue.

I am long or I'm short. I am
grown or I'm bought. I am
painted or I'm bare. I am round
or I'm square. What am I?

Fingernails.

I smell unpleasant when living, but I smell pleasant in death. I am most useful to you, when I stop drawing breath. What am I?

A Pig.

I have two main bodies and I'm

turned all about. When I

standing still, time will run out.

What am I?

An hourglass.

I am light enough to glide the

skies, I am able to show distress

in your eyes. What am I?

Water.

I sit on a bridge, I serve and protect. Removing me is a sign of respect. What am I?

Sunglasses.

I sound like one letter, but I am written with three. I show you things when you look through me. What am I?

An Eye.

I forms holes in my prey, so they

keep their distance. I break

apart, in my threatened

existence. What am I?

An Iceberg.

I have a ring but not one finger to show. Now I follow you whenever you go. What am I?

A Telephone.

I have thirty men, but the women have more powers. They sometimes sit fight for hours. What am I?

A Chess Set.

My mother lives on high and
takes various form, she casts me
away and with winds I am born.
What am I?

Rain.

I have a head and a tail but they will never meet. Having too many of me is always a treat. What am I?

A Coin.

Although I have eyes, I will never use them to see. I live in the dark with my kin, until you have use of me. What am I?

A Potato.

I always make noise but never talk, I always run but never walk, I have a bed but I never sleep, I have a mouth but never speak. What am I?

A river.

I have a neck and two arms, but no head at all. I go with you to work, I go with you to school. What am I?

A shirt.

I travel around the street all day. Or under the bed or by the door I stay. What am I?

Shoes.

Born in the sea and white as

snow. Put me back to water and

away I go. What am I?

Salt.

I have towns with no hope, hills with no slope. I have forests with no trees and a rose with no leaves. What am I?

A Map.

I grow, I get old and I die. I have thousands of siblings and you prefer it when we are dry. What am I?

Hair.

I am a room you cannot enter and you cannot or leave. Rising out of death I do not breathe. I could be your defeat, or a delicious treat. What am I?

A mushroom.

I come in different colors and
many different shapes. Some of
me is curvy and some of me is
straight. I only belong in one
place, but usually I sit in a
darkened space. What am I?

A Jigsaw Piece.

You make use of me from your head to your toe, the more you make me work the thinner I grow. What am I?

A bar of soap.

Though I always stay beneath my roof, I never stay dry, I offer lies and the truth. What am I?

Your tongue.

I could be as white as snow or
as black as soot. I am bought by
the yard but worn by the foot.

Carpet.

Higher I rise, with help from the sun. From my glass cage, I can never run. What am I?

Mercury.

I can never be thrown but I can

be caught. To lose me all kinds

of ways are sought. What am I?

A Cold.

Many have heard me, I am nothing new. I cannot speak back, until spoken to. What am I?

An echo.

I am always around and quite

often forgotten. I am usually

pure but sometimes I'm rotten.

What am I?

Air.

I have no eyes to behold, but I once could see. I once owned thoughts, but now I'm empty. What am I?

A Skull.

I travel from house to house,

wide or tight. Whatever the

weather, I lay outside overnight.

What am I?

A Road.

With pointed fangs and in plain sight, my bloodless victims are bound by my bite. What am I?

A stapler.

I don't have the voice of a person but I can teach you far more. My knowledge is limited, I can never learn more. What am I?

A Book.

I flip everything I see, even

when I stay still. I can either give

you a shock or a thrill. What am

I?

A Mirror.

Kings and queens admire my power, yet I can be held in the hand and make your enemies sour. What am I?

Ace.

The more you remove the

bigger I get, go deep enough

and you're bound to get wet.

What am I?

A hole.

I am the beginning of the end

and I'm in a bend. I am at the

end of the race and the last in

space. What am I?

The letter E.

I dig caves, to store silver and gold. I build bridges for the young, but rarely the old. Everybody needs me, but nobody wants to see me. Who am I?

The Dentist.

Having some, you want more.
But when you have too much, I
may be a bore. What am I?

Money.

I never was but always will be.
No one ever saw or experienced
me. I inspire people to do better
today, and never do I give my
secrets away. What am I?

Tomorrow.

Each any every one you take,

you leave another in your wake.

What am I?

Footsteps.

To people I chain, through ties in the mind. Yet I only touch one of the two that I bind. What am I?

A Wedding Ring.

I am a cold man without a soul.
Burn me and you're sure to
leave a hole. What am I?

A snowman.

I am heavy forward, I weigh a lot. But when I am backwards I'm certainly not. What am I?

A ton.

I can be hidden and a half, I can guide your path. I can shine without fire, I can heighten desire. What am I?

The moon.

With a row of sharp teeth, I bite

all beneath. While I have a

straight back, my brothers can

hack. What am I?

A saw.

In families, I'm known to I run. Passed on from father and mother to son. What am I?

Blood.

Who makes me, has no need of my use. Who uses me, may be at the end of a noose. What am I?

A coffin.

I can't go left, I can't go right. I climb in the day and right through the night. What am I?

An Elevator.

I can bring tears to your eyes,

make you pray to the skies. I

can bring back the dead, or

mess with your head. What am

I?

A memory.

Although glorified, I'm not at my best. Power will fall to me when my father is dead. What am I?

A Prince.

I beam, I shine, I sparkle white.

I'll brighten you day with my

pale light. What am I?

A Smile.

I seem to never get off the hook, I become a person when combined with a book. What am I?

A Worm.

Locked away in a wooden cage,

my teachings are often erased

from page. What am I?

Lead.

I only exist when you are near.

Often seen, but with no voice to

hear. What am I?

Your Reflection.

With only one of me you can't

count past six, nor can this

riddle ever be fixed. What am I?

Syllables.

I live around the world, but I've never been seen. You block me out with a transparent screen.

What am I?

Wind.

I am a silver horse with a flaxen tail. I live to connect, I live to impale. What am I?

A Sewing Needle.

I can't be bought, can't be sold,

even if sometimes, I am made

of gold. What am I?

A Heart.

I have many teeth, but I never could bite. Used early in the day and rarely at night. What am I?

A Comb.

I have six faces and 21 eyes, if I carry a load, I tend to tell lies. What am I?

Dice.

I stare at you and you stare back at me. I have three bright eyes but I cannot see. Every time that I blink, I give you commands. You do what you're told, with your feet and hands. What am I?

A traffic light.

What force and strength cannot

get through, I can easily undo.

What am I?

A Key.

I am an instrument through

which sounds are made, but

nevertheless I cannot be played.

What am I?

A Voice.

After a fall, I will be there. What once was alive, will now be bare. What am I?

Winter.

I always work with something in my eye, but never will you see me cry. What am I?

A Needle.

For some I cause joy, for some I cause strife. Treat me well and I last for life. What am I?

Marriage.

I can only be released from the tunnel when you pull back. I do great damage, when I attack. What am I?

A Bullet.

I am a mother and a sister from a family of eight. I spin all day despite my weight. What am I?

Earth.

Here I sit before your eyes. I help you seek the truth, yet I often give lies. What am I?

Your Brain.

Passed down the tree they come from above. Women take me from my owner when they are in love. What am I?

Last Name.

You throw away my coat and eat my inside. Then once down your throat you throw away my inside. What am I?

Corn on the cob.

If you have more than most,

you're wise, not a fool. For most

animals, I am a useful tool.

What am I?

Teeth.

Pick me up and scratch my head, now I am black where I once was red. What am I?

A Match.

You can touch me, but not see me either way. You can throw me out, but you can't throw me away. What am I?

Your back.

Formed in the darkness but now I shine bright. I am fairly round, and a lady's delight. What am I?

A Pearl.

I usually die before I'm a year old. My mother is tall and my fear is the cold. What am I?

A leaf.

Poor people have much and rich

people do not. If you eat it you

die and I'm not a whole lot.

What is it?

Nothing.

I am a seed with just three letters to my name. Remove the last two and I still sound the same. What am I?

A Pea.

I'm great at concealing what's real and what's true. Sometimes, I can bring out more courage in you. What am I?

Makeup.

I hold with great strength, for something so light. After I enter a hole, everything becomes tight. What am I?

A Screw.

The more you have, the less you will see. Shine a light on me and watch me flee. What am I?

Darkness.

I am a simpleton and I am a child. As you become older my presence gets mild. What am I?

Innocence.

I widen my jaws, two fingers operate me. I cut through my prey so easily. What am I?

Scissors.

With black three eyes I go
where you like, I deal my blow
with one single strike. What am
I?

A Bowling Ball.

I sleep when you wake, I wake

when you dream. No feathers

for flight and silent I seem.

What am I?

A Bat.

Break me in two, I'll continue to tick. Some say that I'm too easy to trick. What am I?

A Heart.

I may only be given but never bought. Saints do not need me, by sinners I'm sought. What am I?

Forgiveness.

At night I come in an vast space

that seems swollen, and by day I

am lost without being stolen.

What am I?

A Star.

I am a ship that can ride into a
new zone. I am built by the
mind, you are never alone.
What am I?

Friendship.

I'm red, blue, purple, and green.
I can never be caught and only
sometimes be seen. What am I?

A Rainbow.

A weight in my gut, trees high

on my back, nails in my ribs ,it's

feet that I lack. What am I?

A ship.

I hurt without moving, I poison without touch. I bear truth and lies, I offer you much. What am I?

Words.

I can be taken back, I am big
and I'm small. If I am broken,
though I fall. What am I?

A deal.

I go up and down in one swift motion. To many I conjuror a childish notion. What am I?

A See-saw.

No matter the shape, I will be in a row. My name has no letters, but my initials are MNO. What am I?

The number 6 on a telephone keypad.

I am the only thing that places

today, far before yesterday.

What am I?

A Dictionary.

I am what no man wants, but

what no man wants to lose.

Those who I defeat, have a

financial bruise.

A lawsuit.

FINAL THOUGHTS

Well, there you have it! 100 riddles, I hope you managed to crack most of them!

Thank you so much for taking a look at this book, I really do appreciate it. If you would also consider taking the time to leave me an honest review on this book on Amazon I would be extremely appreciative of your feedback.

You can find links to all of my books, by simply searching for "Charles Berry" on Amazon. Thanks again for reading and I will hopefully speak to you all in the next book!

37902651R00114

Printed in Great Britain
by Amazon